WITHDRAWN

D1529083

INSIDE ANIMALS

Brimming with creative inspiration, how-to projects, and useful information to enrich your everyday life, Quarto Knows is a favourite destination for those pursuing their interests and passions. Visit our site and dig deeper with our books into your area of interest: Quarto Creates, Quarto Cooks, Quarto Homes, Quarto Lives, Quarto Drives, Quarto Explores, Quarto Gifts, or Quarto Kids.

First published in 2021 by Wide Eyed Editions, an imprint of The Quarto Group. 100 Cummings Center, Suite 265D, Beverly, MA 01915, USA. T +1 978-282-9590 F +1 078-283-2742 **www.QuartoKnows.com**

A catalog record for this book is available from the British Library.

ISBN 978-0-7112-5508-1

The illustrations were created digitally
Set in Vibur, Tango BT and Montserrat

Published by Georgia Amson-Bradshaw
Designed by Myrto Dimitrakoulia
Commissioned by Claire Grace
Edited by Claire Grace and Lucy Menzies
Production by Dawn Cameron

Manufactured in Guangdong, China CC052021

10 9 8 7 6 5 4 3 2 1

INSIDE ANIMALS

Barbara Taylor   Margaux Carpentier

WIDE EYED EDITIONS

CONTENTS

INTRODUCTION

This book takes a look
at some of the most fascinating
animals on Earth—from the inside!

There's so much going on in animal bodies that's
hidden from the naked eye. Some things you'll recognize
from human bodies, such as the brain, heart, and lungs,
but each animal has its own unique insides to help them
survive and thrive in the wild. This means that there are
all kinds of weird and wonderful organs and senses in the
animal kingdom, such as the honey stomach in
a honeybee or the ink sac of an octopus.

From the cow—which has four
stomachs—to the tiny spider—which has
blue blood—you'll discover some truly
amazing facts. Once you've seen these
incredible creature cross sections,
you'll never look at animals
in the same way again!

RATTLESNAKE

Muscles

A snake's muscles are very powerful. They help it to move, protect its soft organs, and push food into its stomach and down to its intestines.

Rattle

A rattlesnake shakes the "rattle" at the end of its tail to warn predators to keep away. The rattle is made of old tail tips. Each time the rattlesnake sheds its skin, it adds another layer to its rattle.

Inner ear

Even though they don't have ears, snakes can hear. Inside their head is a special bone that can feel sounds being made around them.

INTESTINE

KIDNEY

INSIDE... A SNAKE

Snakes spend their lives slithering across the ground. These reptiles have a dry skin covered in tough scales, which protects them like a suit of armor. As snakes grow, they shed their skin several times a year.

Tongue

Like all snakes, a rattlesnake's tongue is "forked," meaning split in two at the tip. Snakes use their tongues to smell. They stick out their tongue and lick smells from the air. Then an organ in their mouth tells the snake what that smell belongs to.

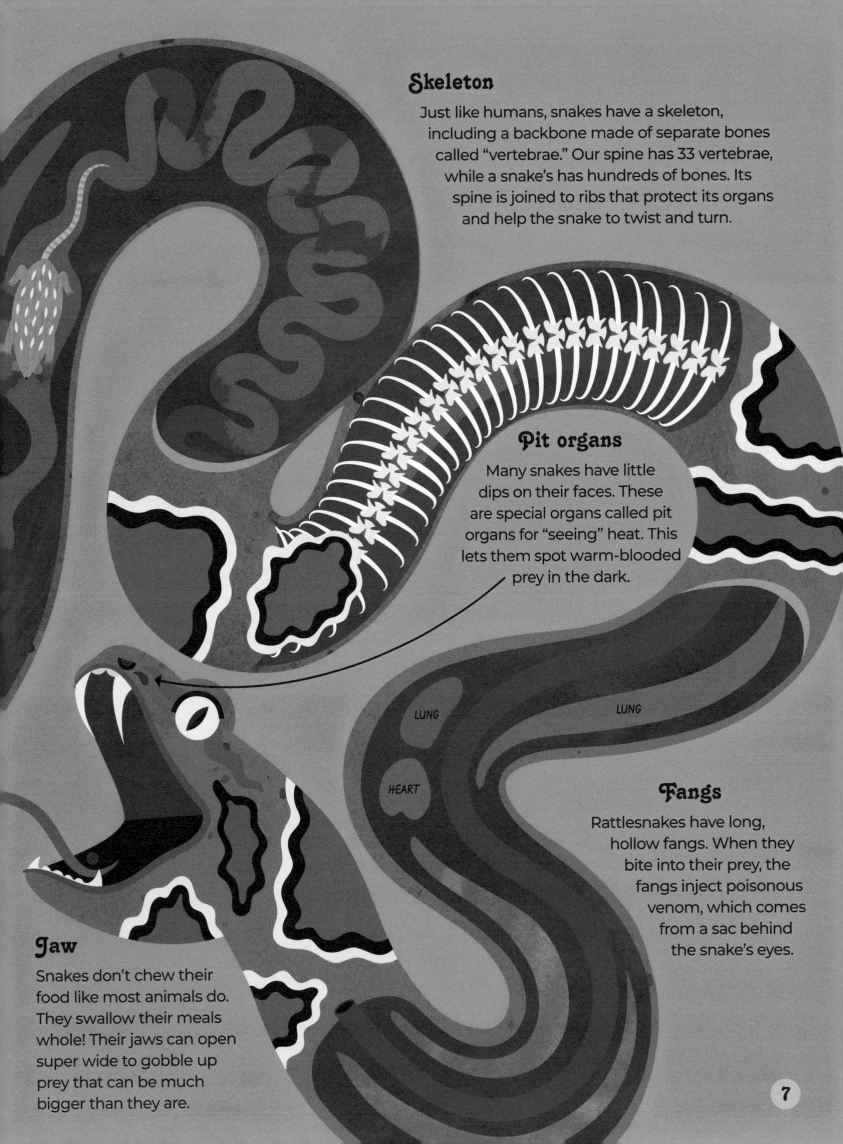

Skeleton

Just like humans, snakes have a skeleton, including a backbone made of separate bones called "vertebrae." Our spine has 33 vertebrae, while a snake's has hundreds of bones. Its spine is joined to ribs that protect its organs and help the snake to twist and turn.

Pit organs

Many snakes have little dips on their faces. These are special organs called pit organs for "seeing" heat. This lets them spot warm-blooded prey in the dark.

LUNG

LUNG

HEART

Fangs

Rattlesnakes have long, hollow fangs. When they bite into their prey, the fangs inject poisonous venom, which comes from a sac behind the snake's eyes.

Jaw

Snakes don't chew their food like most animals do. They swallow their meals whole! Their jaws can open super wide to gobble up prey that can be much bigger than they are.

INSIDE... A CAMEL

People have ridden camels as a form of transportation for thousands of years. There are two different species: the dromedary camel, which has one hump on its back, and this, the Bactrian camel, which has two humps. Camels can survive for months without food, can carry up to 440 pounds on their backs and can walk for up to 25 miles in the hot desert sun.

Humps

Camel humps store fat, which can be broken down to provide energy when food is scarce.

SMALL INTESTINE

LARGE INTESTINE

Stomach

Camels have one stomach that is split into three parts called "chambers." They throw up their food and eat it again so they can easily digest it.

Feet

Camels' feet look like two big toes. They are very broad and have a little pad, like a cushion, underneath. This helps them walk on soft sand without sinking or slipping.

Eyes

To keep out sand and dust, camels have two sets of extra-long eyelashes per eye, plus a thin barrier called a "membrane" that covers each eyeball.

Nostrils

Amazingly, camels can actually close their nostrils so that sand won't get in.

Spit

If a camel is angry or in danger, it will spit at whatever is bothering it. The spit contains food from the camel's stomach, so it is more like throwing up!

HEART

Neck

Camels can grow to over six feet tall. That's taller than most adults! Their long, curved necks let them reach food on the ground.

BACTRIAN CAMEL

INSIDE... A SHARK

There are over 500 known kinds of shark. Sharks live in every ocean in the world, whether shallow or deep, warm or cold, clear or murky. A few even live in rivers and lakes. With little teethlike points that make water flow smoothly over their skin, sharks can swim very fast. The great white shark is the largest fish that hunts other animals. It can swim at over 37 miles per hour!

Muscles

Sharks have two layers of muscle: red on the surface and white underneath. The red muscles help them swim for longer. The white muscles make them quick and agile.

Spiral valve

This organ slows down the movement of food so the shark can absorb as much nutrition as possible.

Liver

A shark's liver is very large. It is full of oil that helps the shark float because oil is less dense (lighter) than water.

Teeth

Most sharks have rows and rows of sharp, pointy teeth. Just like humans, sharks' teeth fall out over time. But unlike humans, sharks grow new teeth for their whole life. A great white shark can have seven rows of teeth and 300 teeth at any one time.

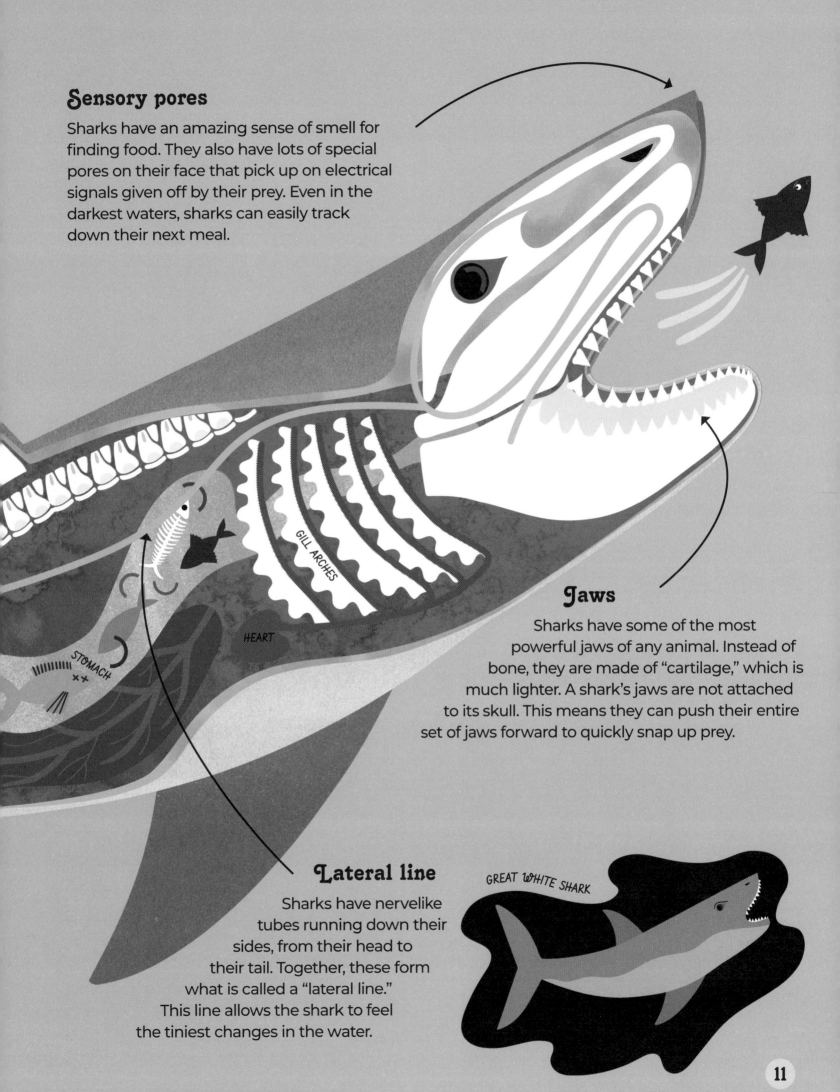

Sensory pores

Sharks have an amazing sense of smell for finding food. They also have lots of special pores on their face that pick up on electrical signals given off by their prey. Even in the darkest waters, sharks can easily track down their next meal.

GILL ARCHES

HEART

STOMACH

Jaws

Sharks have some of the most powerful jaws of any animal. Instead of bone, they are made of "cartilage," which is much lighter. A shark's jaws are not attached to its skull. This means they can push their entire set of jaws forward to quickly snap up prey.

Lateral line

Sharks have nervelike tubes running down their sides, from their head to their tail. Together, these form what is called a "lateral line." This line allows the shark to feel the tiniest changes in the water.

GREAT WHITE SHARK

11

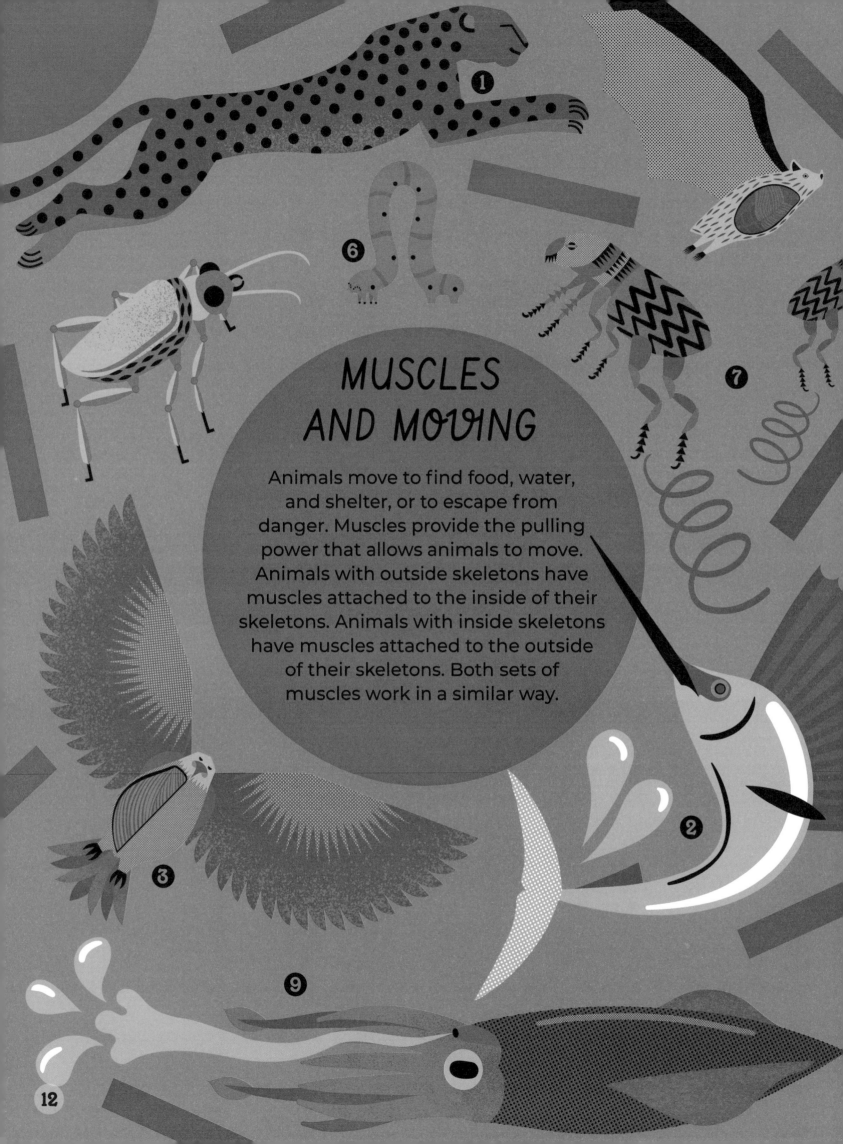

MUSCLES AND MOVING

Animals move to find food, water, and shelter, or to escape from danger. Muscles provide the pulling power that allows animals to move. Animals with outside skeletons have muscles attached to the inside of their skeletons. Animals with inside skeletons have muscles attached to the outside of their skeletons. Both sets of muscles work in a similar way.

❶ Speedy cheetah

A cheetah uses its powerful leg and spine muscles to reach speeds of 39 mph in just three giant strides! It has to stop after about 20 seconds though—it gets too hot!

❷ Fastest fish

The fastest fish in the sea are the sailfish and the marlin, which use their muscles to whiz along at over 62 mph. These speedy fish are a pointy, streamlined shape to slide through the water easily.

❸ Flying power

An eagle has powerful chest muscles to flap its huge wings up and down. These muscles are joined to a large, flat part of its breastbone, called the keel. Eagles are the strongest birds in the world.

❹ Foot muscle

A snail slides along on one big, slimy muscle called a foot. The foot muscle gets shorter and longer in waves, from the back to the front of the snail's foot. The slime helps the snail to glide easily over rough surfaces.

❺ How muscles work

Muscles work by making themselves shorter, which is usually triggered by nerve signals. This pulls part of the animal's body into a different position. When the muscles relax, the body moves back to its original position.

❻ Looping

Some caterpillars are called "loopers" because they pull their bodies into a loop as they creep slowly along. This is because they have no legs along the middle of their body.

❼ High jumpers

Fleas store energy in pads at the base of their legs. These pads suddenly flick the flea's back legs to catapult it into the air. For their size, fleas can jump higher than any other animal!

❽ Joints

A joint is where the hard parts of a skeleton meet. Joints allow bones, or the tough plates of an exoskeleton, to bend.

❾ Jet propulsion

Squid and octopuses suck water into a muscular chamber inside their body. Then they squirt out the water through a tube called a siphon to push themselves backward very fast.

Did you know?

About 60 percent of a horse's weight is made up of muscle.

A snail can slide over a sharp knife without hurting itself because of its thick slime.

If you could jump as high as a flea, you would be able to jump over a house!

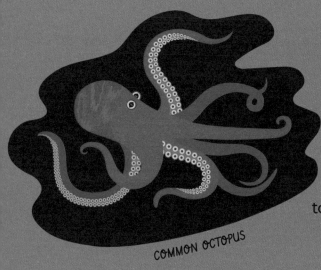

COMMON OCTOPUS

Brain

Octopuses are smart! They can use tools, find their way through mazes, play with Rubik's cubes, and solve puzzles. Some scientists think that octopuses can even tell different humans apart.

Mantle

Most of an octopus's organs are behind its head in a part of its body called the "mantle." They don't have skeletons, but some have a tough casing around their organs to keep them safe.

Heart

An octopus has three hearts. Two of the hearts pump blood to their gills. The third heart pumps blood to the rest of the body. When octopuses swim, their third heart stops beating and they get tired. This is why they often crawl on the ocean floor.

LIVER

KIDNEY

GILL

Camouflaging skin

Octopuses have special skin that lets them change color to match their surroundings. They use this to hide when predators are around.

INSIDE... AN OCTOPUS

Octopuses have eight arms and can be found in all of the world's oceans. Their bodies are soft so they can squeeze through tiny spaces. If an octopus loses an arm, it can just grow it back! The biggest octopuses are around 16 feet long—bigger than some cars—and the smallest are around one inch long.

Ink

Octopuses store ink in their "ink sacs," and shoot it out through tubes called "siphons." The ink confuses predators so that the octopus can escape from danger.

Blood

An octopus's blood is blue! This is because it has lots of copper in it. Copper helps oxygen move around its body, especially in cold water.

Suckers

Humans use their tongue to taste things. But not octopuses! They use hundreds of little suckers on their eight arms to taste and smell anything they touch.

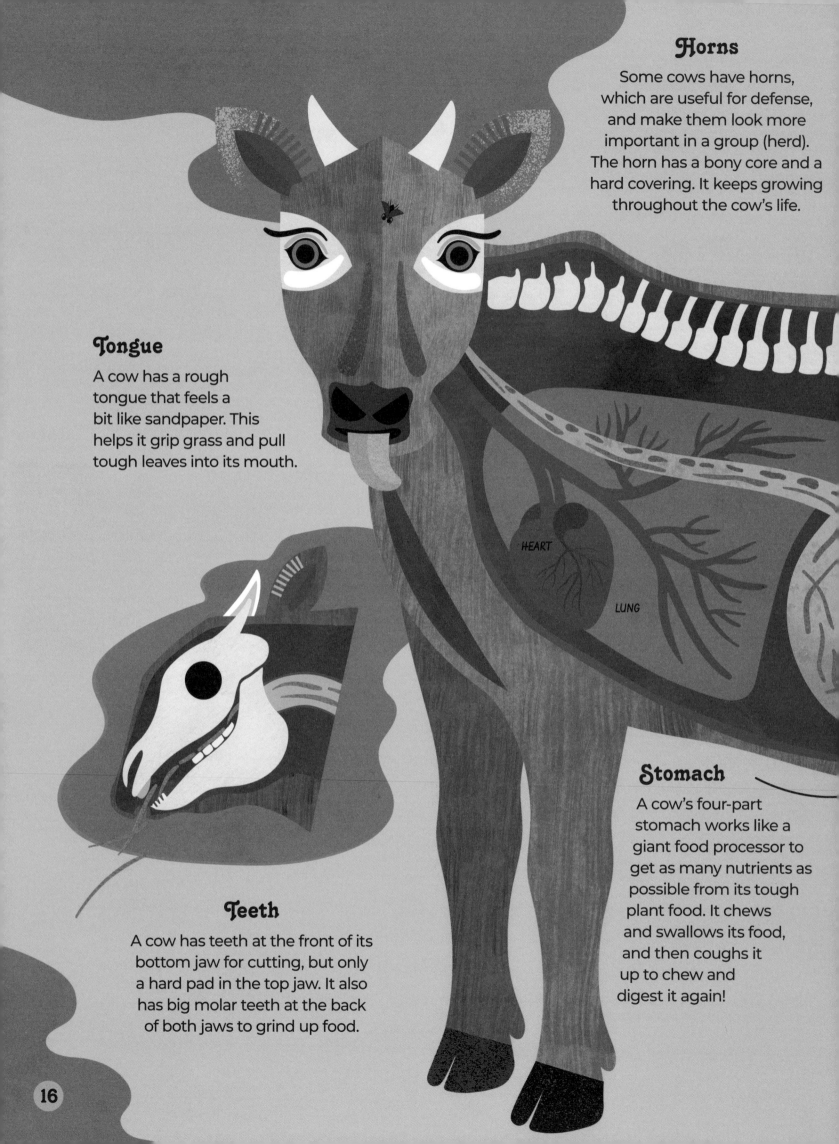

Horns

Some cows have horns, which are useful for defense, and make them look more important in a group (herd). The horn has a bony core and a hard covering. It keeps growing throughout the cow's life.

Tongue

A cow has a rough tongue that feels a bit like sandpaper. This helps it grip grass and pull tough leaves into its mouth.

HEART

LUNG

Stomach

A cow's four-part stomach works like a giant food processor to get as many nutrients as possible from its tough plant food. It chews and swallows its food, and then coughs it up to chew and digest it again!

Teeth

A cow has teeth at the front of its bottom jaw for cutting, but only a hard pad in the top jaw. It also has big molar teeth at the back of both jaws to grind up food.

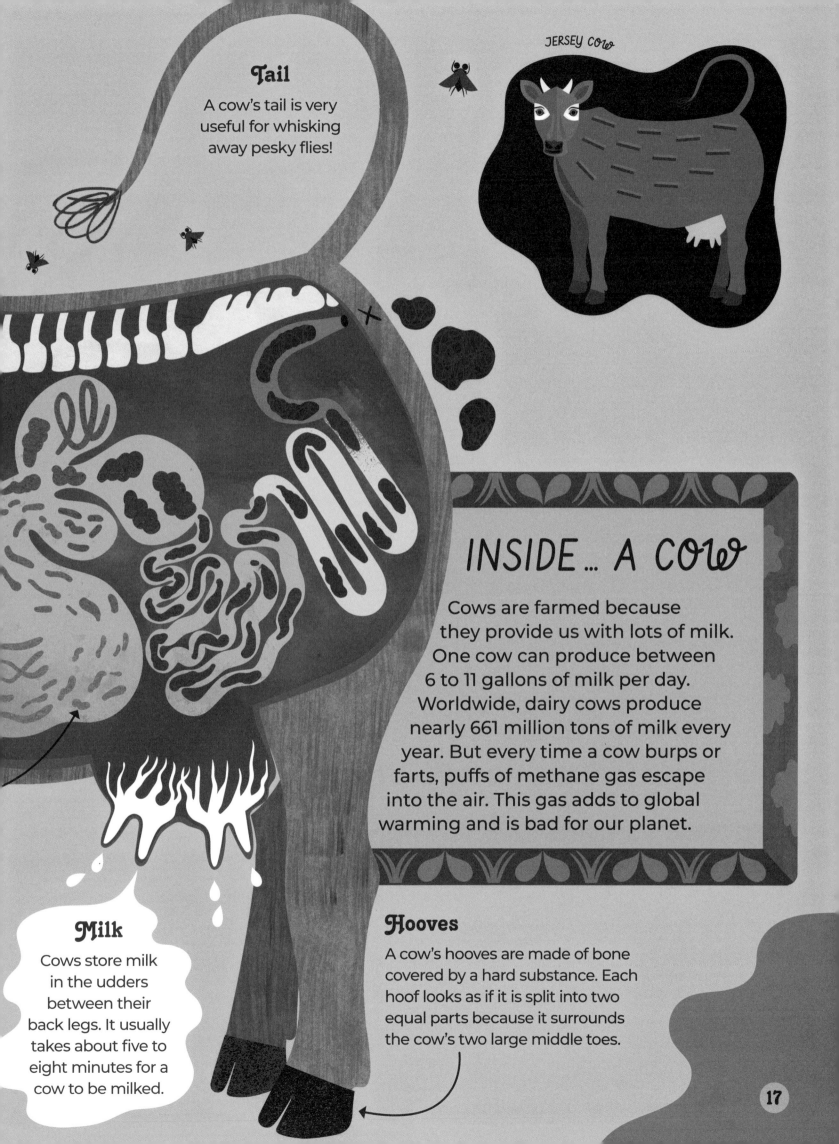

Tail

A cow's tail is very useful for whisking away pesky flies!

JERSEY COW

INSIDE... A COW

Cows are farmed because they provide us with lots of milk. One cow can produce between 6 to 11 gallons of milk per day. Worldwide, dairy cows produce nearly 661 million tons of milk every year. But every time a cow burps or farts, puffs of methane gas escape into the air. This gas adds to global warming and is bad for our planet.

Milk

Cows store milk in the udders between their back legs. It usually takes about five to eight minutes for a cow to be milked.

Hooves

A cow's hooves are made of bone covered by a hard substance. Each hoof looks as if it is split into two equal parts because it surrounds the cow's two large middle toes.

Enormous eyes

An ostrich has eyes the size of tennis balls—the largest eyes of any land animal. Each eyeball is bigger than its brain! Keen eyesight helps an ostrich to spot danger from a long way away.

Grinding food

Like all birds, ostriches have no teeth to chew their food. So they swallow sand and pebbles that help to grind up the food inside a small pouch called the gizzard. The gizzard is next to the stomach.

STOMACH

AIR SAC

Breathing

Ostriches need plenty of oxygen when they run at high speeds. Like flying birds, they breathe through very efficient lungs that take lots of oxygen from the air, as well as a system of air sacs.

AIR SAC

AIR SAC

AIR SAC

AIR SAC

AIR SAC

Long legs

Ostriches have muscular legs up to four feet long, which allows these big birds to reach incredible speeds. Their legs are also weapons—ostriches can kill lions or people with their sharp claws and deadly kicks.

Two toes

Most birds have four toes on each foot, but an ostrich has only two toes. One big toe has a nail like a hoof and supports the weight of the ostrich. A smaller toe has no nail and is used for balance.

INSIDE ... AN OSTRICH

The world's largest living bird is the ostrich, which is tall enough to look over the heads of most adults. Ostriches are much too heavy to fly. They can, however, run faster than a racehorse and cover a distance of up to 16 feet with just one stride. Their tiny wings help them to balance when sprinting away from predators, such as lions, leopards, and hyenas.

Feathers

Unlike other birds, an ostrich's feathers don't hook together. This makes them look fluffy and shaggy. These feathers keep the bird warm. Males also display their wing feathers to attract females.

Intestine

The intestine of an ostrich is about 45 feet long—about twice as long as a human's. It takes about three days for food to pass through the intestine, allowing as much nutrients as possible to be taken from the tough plants that an ostrich eats.

Egg

The ostrich lays the biggest egg in the world. One ostrich egg is equivalent to the weight of about 24 chicken eggs. The shell is so strong that an adult human could stand on it... and it wouldn't break!

COMMON OSTRICH

19

SKELETONS

A skeleton is the strong framework that supports an animal's body, helps it to move, and protects its soft internal organs, such as its heart or lungs. Most animals either have a skeleton inside or outside their bodies, but some animals have both. A skeleton is usually made of a hard material, such as bone or chitin.

1 Squishy skeletons

Some animals don't have a hard skeleton at all. Instead, muscles squeeze fluids inside their bodies to create a soft, skeleton-like structure. This means they can fit through small spaces but their bodies are not very strong. Animals such as jellyfish, sea anemones, octopuses, and earthworms have squishy skeletons like this.

2 Outside skeletons

Many animals have skeletons that are outside their bodies. Snails and crabs have shells, starfish have spiny cases, and insects and spiders have tough body armor.

3 Bony skeletons

Many animals have an internal skeleton made of bone. There are about 206 bones in a human's skeleton, but a large snake, such as a python, can have up to 1,800 bones inside its body!

4 Rubbery skeletons

The skeletons of over 1,000 different kinds of fish, including sharks, skates, and rays, are made of strong, rubbery cartilage instead of bone. This makes their skeletons lighter, so they can move faster to catch prey and avoid predators.

5 Two skeletons

Some animals have skeletons both inside and outside their bodies. This provides extra protection but restricts movement. A turtle has an inner skeleton as well as a shell that protects its vital organs

6 Shells

The hard outer shell of shellfish and snails is made from calcium carbonate, or chalk. A land snail can pull its body inside its shell to escape danger, or to survive hot or cold weather.

7 Teeth and jaws

The teeth and jaws in an animal's jaw bone are used for cutting and grinding food, catching prey, and for defense. A beaver's teeth are strong enough to cut down trees!

8 Bird bones

Many of a bird's bones are hollow, with a honeycomb of air spaces inside to help them get enough oxygen for flying. Birds have horny beaks instead of heavy jaw bones and teeth, which would make them too heavy to take off.

Did you know?

A seahorse doesn't have ribs. Its outer skeleton gives it extra protection and support.

The grizzly bear's jaws and teeth are strong enough to crush a bowling ball.

The Great Barrier Reef of Australia is made from the skeletons of millions of coral animals.

Black and white

On land, a penguin's black back soaks up the sun's warmth, while its white front reflects heat away to keep it cool. In the ocean, the black and white colors help to camouflage a penguin from predators.

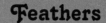

Feathers

Penguins have more feathers than most other birds. Their small, stiff outer feathers are tightly packed together and stop the wind blowing warmth away from its body. The fluffy base of the feathers traps body heat, like a quilt. Penguins create an oil to spread over their feathers to keep them waterproof.

Heavy bones

A penguin's bones are solid and heavy, which help it to dive under the water. The bones inside its paddlelike flippers are wide and flat to push water aside easily.

INTESTINE

INSIDE... A PENGUIN

Zooming along underwater at speeds faster than an Olympic swimmer, the streamlined body of a penguin is superbly adapted to "flying" underwater. Penguins spend up to three-quarters of their lives in the ocean. Millions of years ago, there were giant penguins as big as an adult human. Today, the biggest penguin, the emperor, is only as tall as a small child.

Warm layer

Penguins have a thick blanket of fat—called blubber—under their skin to keep them warm in cold water. The fat is also a useful store of energy and protects penguins from knocks and bumps on land.

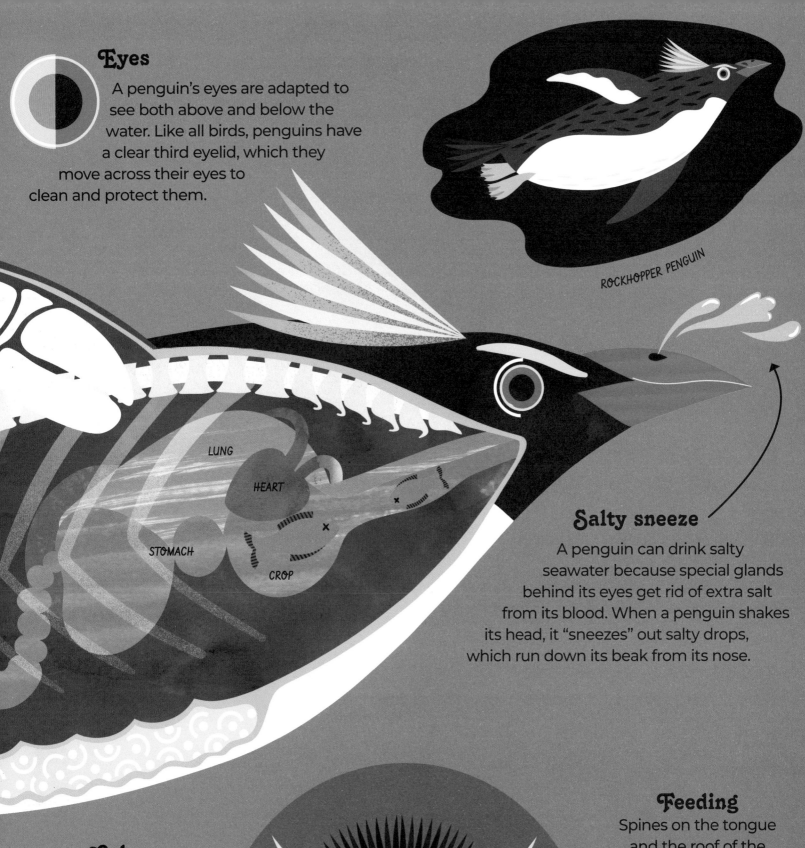

Eyes

A penguin's eyes are adapted to see both above and below the water. Like all birds, penguins have a clear third eyelid, which they move across their eyes to clean and protect them.

ROCKHOPPER PENGUIN

LUNG

HEART

STOMACH

CROP

Salty sneeze

A penguin can drink salty seawater because special glands behind its eyes get rid of extra salt from its blood. When a penguin shakes its head, it "sneezes" out salty drops, which run down its beak from its nose.

Color and crests

The colors, patterns, or crests on penguins' heads are used for display and courtship, and help penguins recognize each other. Rockhopper penguins have crests that look like long eyebrows.

Feeding

Spines on the tongue and the roof of the mouth help penguins to grip slippery prey, such as fish. Parent penguins store the seafood they catch in their crop—a part of their stomach— and cough it up for their chicks back on land.

INSIDE ... A GORILLA

Rare, intelligent and peaceful vegetarians, gorillas are members of the great ape family. They are one of our closest cousins, with insides very similar to ours. They also have nails and unique fingerprints, as we do. Gorillas are, however, up to six times stronger than a person and have a more muscular, hairy body, with a big belly for digesting their plant food.

Fur

A gorilla's fur helps to keep it warm. Mountain gorillas have longer, thicker fur, because they live in cold places. A male gorilla grows silver hair on his back when he grows up, which makes him look bigger. He is then called a silverback.

Big belly

The large belly of a gorilla is bigger than its chest. This allows room for its extra-long, coiled intestines and helps it to digest the bulky plants in its diet. A gorilla spends much of its time eating and has a varied diet of more than 200 different plants.

SHOULDER BLADE

LUNG

STOMACH

INTESTINE

Fingers

A gorilla's fingers are much thicker than yours—about as thick as bananas! Its thumbs can press against each finger, so it can either grasp things firmly, or hold them delicately.

Bones

Gorilla bones are much more solid and stronger than human bones, so they are less likely to break. But the weight of their bones means gorillas are too heavy to swim.

Brain

A gorilla has a large head, with a well-developed brain inside. Gorillas can learn sign language, but their vocal cords do not allow them to speak. The gorilla's brain is smaller than ours—about one-third as big as the human brain.

Grooming

The gorillas in a group regularly search through each other's fur with their fingers. This keeps their fur clean and also relaxes the gorillas, helping them to stay friends.

Teeth

Gorillas have the same number of teeth as we have—32. They also grow two full sets of teeth. Their baby teeth fall out and are replaced by permanent adult teeth. Large molar teeth, attached to strong muscles, grind up the tough plants they eat.

Arms and legs

A gorilla's arms are longer than its legs. This helps it to walk on all fours, rather than walking upright like a human. It curls up its fingers when it walks, so its bony knuckles hold the weight of its body.

MOUNTAIN GORILLA

INSIDE... A PARROT

There are over 350 species of parrots, ranging in size from a finger-sized pygmy parrot to the chunky, flightless kakapo. The biggest parrots, such as this scarlet macaw, live for 35–50 years or more. These noisy, intelligent birds are good at copying sounds and can be trained to speak, although they usually do not know what they are saying.

Bendy neck

A parrot has ten bones in its neck—three more than you! This makes its neck very flexible, allowing it to turn its head right over its shoulder without moving its body. A bendy neck helps parrots to spot food or predators.

Preening

Parrots spread an oily liquid over their feathers with their bills to keep them waterproof and in good condition. This oily liquid is made at the base of the parrot's tail.

LUNG

HEART

AIR SAC

LIVER

STOMACH

Toes

Two toes pointing forward and two toes pointing backward gives parrots a powerful grip. This helps them to use their feet for climbing and holding things. Parrots are the only birds that use their feet to hold food up to their bills.

Big bill

A parrot's sharp, curved bill is very strong—perfect for cracking open tough nuts and seeds, and digging nesting holes in trees and soft rocks. It uses its strong tongue to remove flesh from the shells of fruits and nuts.

Colorful feathers

A parrot has between 2,000 and 3,000 feathers! Parrots make their own red, orange, and yellow feather pigments instead of getting these colors from their food, like most other birds. The red colors help to protect their feathers from being damaged by bacteria.

Breathing

Like all flying birds, parrots need a lot of energy for flight. They have air sacs as well as lungs so that air keeps flowing through the body, supplying the oxygen needed to release energy from their food.

Senses

Parrots have keen eyesight and can see all the colors we can see, as well as ultraviolet light, which is invisible to us. Both of these things help them to recognize their mates and friends and enables a group of parrots to stay together in a flock.

SCARLET MACAW

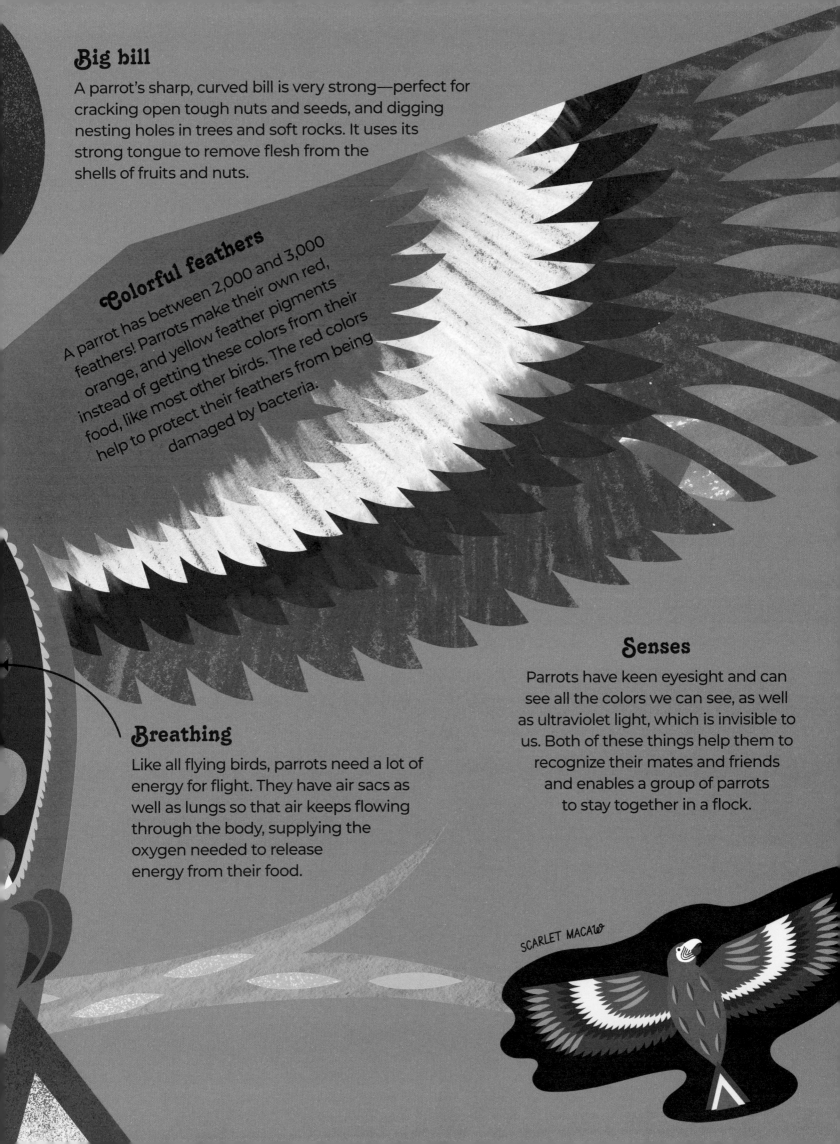

LUNGS AND BREATHING

All animals use oxygen to release energy from their food. Some small animals take in oxygen through the whole surface of their body. Insects use a system of tiny air tubes. Larger animals, such as sharks or elephants, have special organs, such as gills or lungs, to help them breathe in enough oxygen.

① Lungs

Inside an animal's lungs are thousands of tubes leading to tiny air sacs. These air sacs have very thin walls so that oxygen can easily pass into the blood, which carries oxygen around the animal's body.

② Air sacs

Birds have several large air sacs, which are linked to their lungs. This helps them to get the most oxygen from each breath they take, allowing them to release the extra energy they need for flying.

③ Gills

Most animals that live in water, such as fish or oysters, breathe through stacks of thin flaps called gills. The gills are usually red because they contain lots of blood to pick up the oxygen.

④ Skin-breathing

Some of the animals that breathe through their skin, such as earthworms, live on land. Others, such as salamanders or eels, live both in water and on land. These animals need to keep their thin skin moist in order for their skin-breathing system to work on land.

⑤ Breathing out of water

Mudskippers trap pools of water in their gills so they can breathe on land. This makes them look as if they have puffed up cheeks! Mudskippers can also breathe through their skin and the lining of their mouths.

⑥ Insects

A network of tiny air pipes, called tracheae, carry oxygen through an insect's body. The tracheae take in air through small holes in the insect's body casing, called spiracles. A ring of muscle around the spiracles allows them to be opened or closed.

⑦ Snorkels

Water bugs, such as water scorpions and mosquito larvae, take in air at the surface of the water through a breathing tube. This works like snorkels that divers use for breathing at the surface of the water.

⑧ Lungfish

Lungfish are the only fish to breathe through both gills and lungs. When the pools that the lungfish live in dry up, they breathe through their lungs instead of their gills.

⑨ Diving

People can usually hold their breath underwater for about two minutes. Record-breaking human free-divers can make dives lasting up to 24 minutes! This beats the beaver, which can hold its breath underwater for about 15 minutes.

Did you know?

Cuvier's beaked whale holds the record for the longest dive for a mammal. It can stay underwater for over two hours before it has to come up for air!

The breathing tube of a needle bug is almost as long as its entire body!

Ice fish don't have scales, unlike most other fish. This may help them to absorb the oxygen they need directly through their skin.

INSIDE... A CROCODILE

Crocodiles are some of the closest living relatives of the dinosaurs! These fierce hunters all have powerful jaws full of tough, pointy teeth. One crocodile, the saltwater crocodile, is the largest living reptile in the world. It weighs at least twice as much as a grand piano!

Scaly skin

A suit of scaly armor protects and camouflages a crocodile's body. As a crocodile grows bigger, the old scales, called scutes, drop off one at a time and new, bigger scutes take their place.

STOMACH

Stomach stones

Crocodiles swallow pebbles and other hard objects, which swirl around inside part of their stomach. This helps to break down food and release its nutrients.

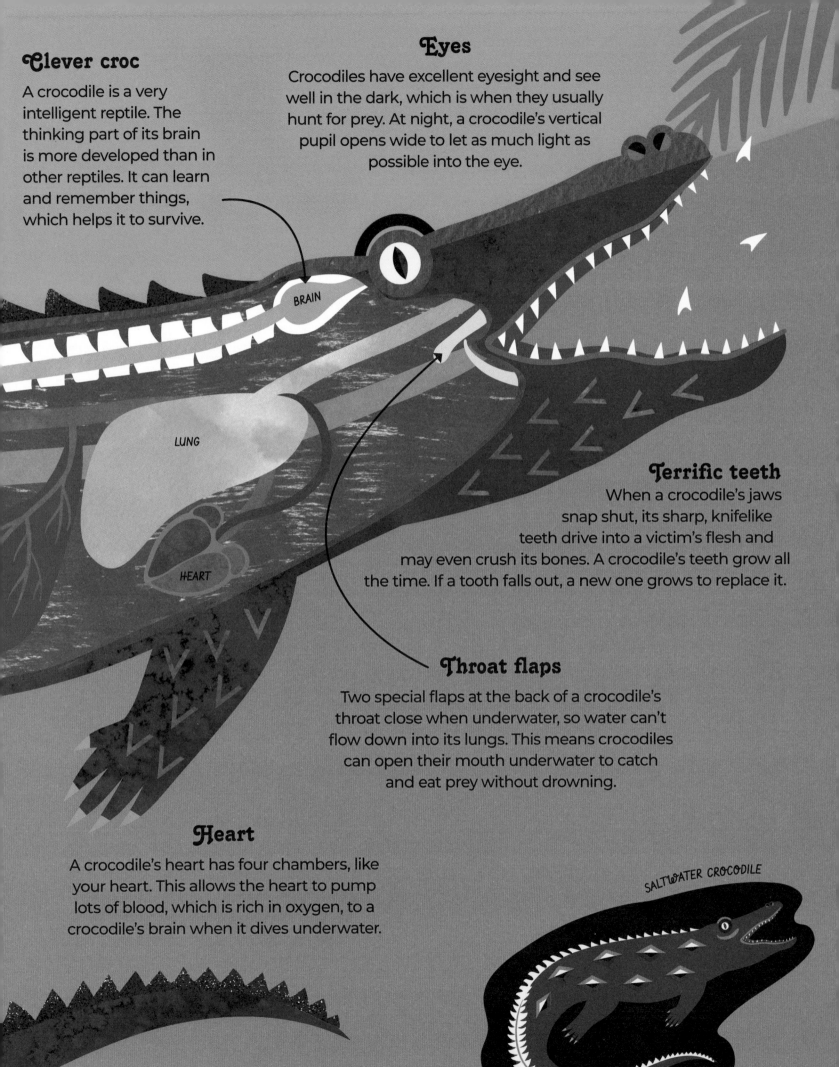

Clever croc

A crocodile is a very intelligent reptile. The thinking part of its brain is more developed than in other reptiles. It can learn and remember things, which helps it to survive.

Eyes

Crocodiles have excellent eyesight and see well in the dark, which is when they usually hunt for prey. At night, a crocodile's vertical pupil opens wide to let as much light as possible into the eye.

BRAIN

LUNG

HEART

Terrific teeth

When a crocodile's jaws snap shut, its sharp, knifelike teeth drive into a victim's flesh and may even crush its bones. A crocodile's teeth grow all the time. If a tooth falls out, a new one grows to replace it.

Throat flaps

Two special flaps at the back of a crocodile's throat close when underwater, so water can't flow down into its lungs. This means crocodiles can open their mouth underwater to catch and eat prey without drowning.

Heart

A crocodile's heart has four chambers, like your heart. This allows the heart to pump lots of blood, which is rich in oxygen, to a crocodile's brain when it dives underwater.

SALTWATER CROCODILE

Nose leaf

Some bats have a fleshy flap on their face called a nose leaf. It's probably to direct the sounds they make, although no one is really sure how this works. Greater horseshoe bats like this one are named after the shape of their nose leaves.

Ears and echoes

Most bats navigate and find prey in the dark by building up a "sound picture" of their surroundings. They send out bursts of very high-pitched sounds through their mouth or nose and wait for the echoes to bounce back to their ears.

Digestion

Bats digest their food very quickly. Only 30–60 minutes after feeding, they start pooping to get rid of undigested food. This reduces the weight they carry around when they fly.

GREATER HORSESHOE BAT

Wings

A bat's wings are made of two layers of skin stretched over its long arm and finger bones. The wings are very flexible and can change shape easily. This helps a bat to weave and dive quickly in the air as it hunts for its prey.

Hanging out

Bats hang upside down to rest or sleep. The strong claws on their feet lock into position so bats can relax and save energy. It also helps them hide from predators.

INSIDE ... A BAT

Bats are the only mammals in the world that can fly. There are over 1,300 different kinds of bat, ranging from a tiny bumblebee-sized bat to giant fruit bats. Most bats come out at night and feed on insects—the brown bat can eat up to 1,000 small insects in just one hour!

Do bats get dizzy?

Bats don't get dizzy hanging upside down because they are small, with less blood than we have, so gravity doesn't make as much blood rush to their head. Valves in their blood vessels also stop blood from rushing to their head.

Bones

The thin, hollow bones of a bat's skeleton are perfect for flying because they are so light. The wing bones are strong and stiff to support the wings during flight.

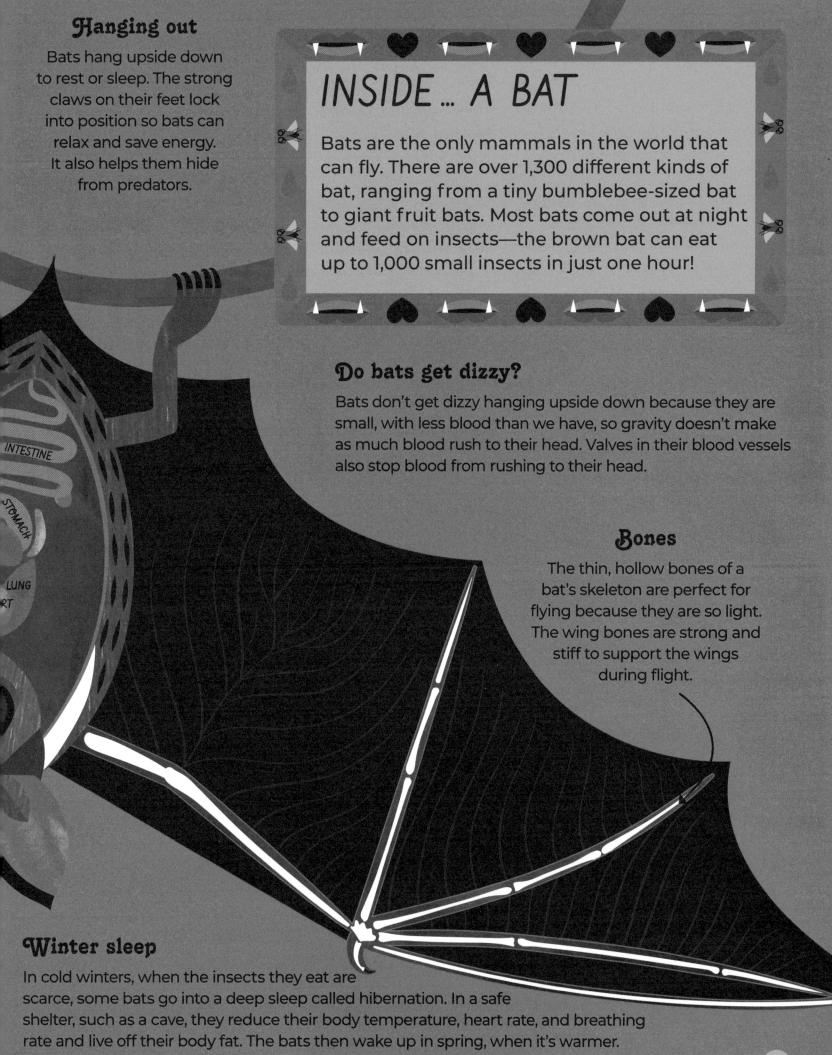

INTESTINE

STOMACH

LUNG

Winter sleep

In cold winters, when the insects they eat are scarce, some bats go into a deep sleep called hibernation. In a safe shelter, such as a cave, they reduce their body temperature, heart rate, and breathing rate and live off their body fat. The bats then wake up in spring, when it's warmer.

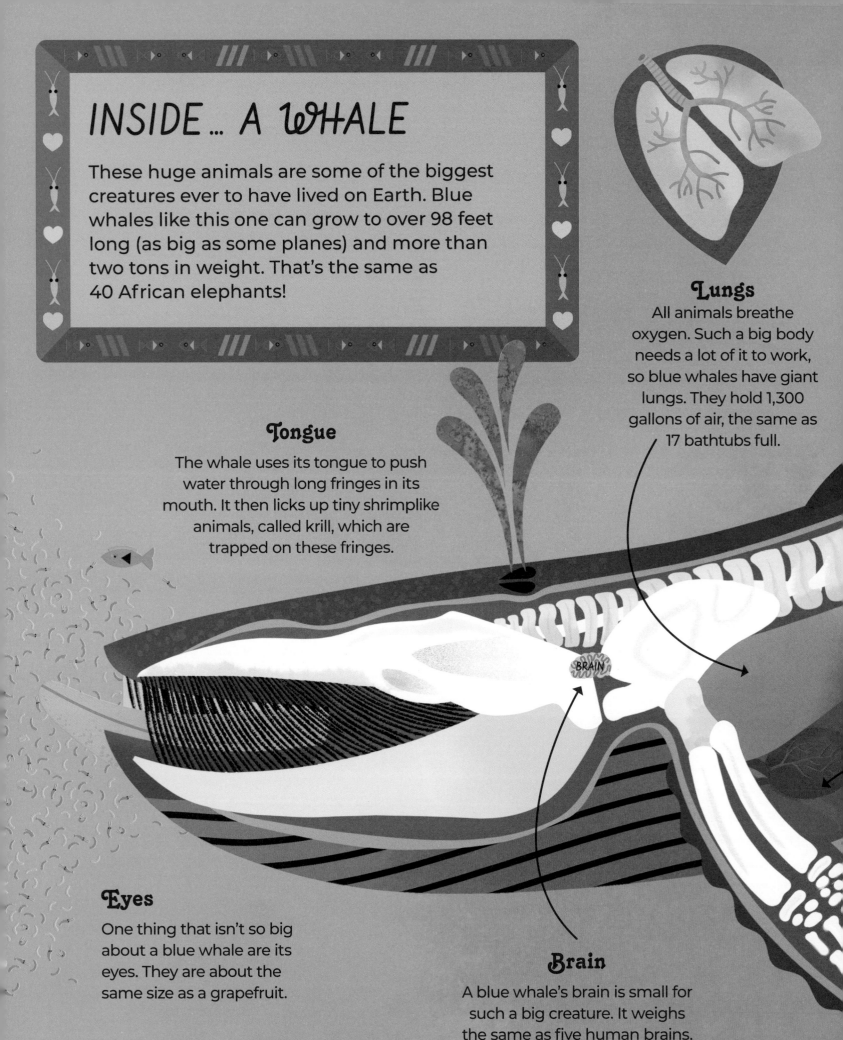

INSIDE... A WHALE

These huge animals are some of the biggest creatures ever to have lived on Earth. Blue whales like this one can grow to over 98 feet long (as big as some planes) and more than two tons in weight. That's the same as 40 African elephants!

Lungs

All animals breathe oxygen. Such a big body needs a lot of it to work, so blue whales have giant lungs. They hold 1,300 gallons of air, the same as 17 bathtubs full.

Tongue

The whale uses its tongue to push water through long fringes in its mouth. It then licks up tiny shrimplike animals, called krill, which are trapped on these fringes.

Eyes

One thing that isn't so big about a blue whale are its eyes. They are about the same size as a grapefruit.

Brain

A blue whale's brain is small for such a big creature. It weighs the same as five human brains.

BRAIN

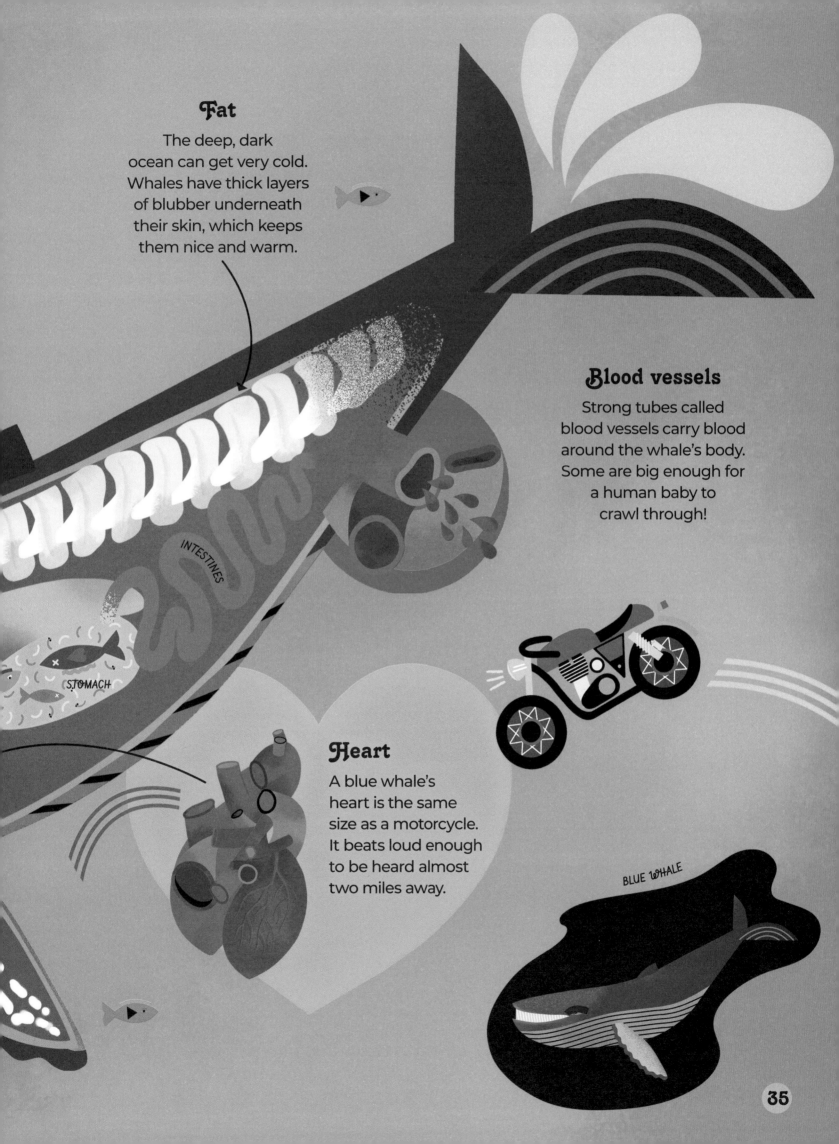

Fat

The deep, dark ocean can get very cold. Whales have thick layers of blubber underneath their skin, which keeps them nice and warm.

Blood vessels

Strong tubes called blood vessels carry blood around the whale's body. Some are big enough for a human baby to crawl through!

INTESTINES

STOMACH

Heart

A blue whale's heart is the same size as a motorcycle. It beats loud enough to be heard almost two miles away.

BLUE WHALE

BRAIN AND SENSES

Animals rely on their sight, hearing, smell, taste, and touch to gather information about their own body and their surroundings. These senses send electrical signals along nerves. The nerves may be linked to a brain, which controls how animals' bodies work.

Animals without backbones

Some animals without backbones, such as starfish or jellyfish, have a simple network of nerves. Others, such as worms or insects, have bunches of nerves, called ganglia, as well as a small brain and a nerve net. A few animals without backbones, such as octopuses or squid, have a well-developed brain and are intelligent animals.

Animals with backbones

All animals with backbones have complex nervous systems, which includes a brain, a bundle of nerves called a spinal cord (inside the backbone), and a branching network of nerves. Some parts of the nervous system, such as some muscles, work automatically, while other parts are under the control of the brain.

❶ Control center

An animal's brain is the control center of its nervous system. A bit like a living computer, a brain receives information, processes it, and sends out messages that control the body's activities. Large animals tend to have big brains to control their large bodies.

❷ Lots of lenses

Animals such as insects and crabs have compound eyes—eyes with lots of lenses. Each lens detects light from a small part of the animal's surroundings. The brain combines all these images to make a complete picture.

❸ Hearing sounds

Sound is made up of vibrations that travel through air, water, or solid objects. Some animals sense these vibrations by hearing them. The ears convert the vibrations into nerve signals that are sent to the animal's brain.

❹ Insect feelers

Insects have threadlike structures, called antennae, sticking out of their head. The antennae are covered in sensitive hairs and are able to pick up air movements, sound vibrations, and smells.

❺ Sensing electricity

The rubbery bill of the platypus detects the movement and electrical signals given off by the nerves in its prey, such as shrimp. This helps it to hunt in muddy water, where it is hard to see clearly.

❻ Touch

For animals that come out at night or live underground, such as moles, touch is a very important sense. The star-nosed mole is named after the starlike tentacles on its nose, which have 100,000 nerves going to the mole's brain.

Did you know?

The tongue of a rabbit contains 17,000 taste buds.

The brain of a bee is only a millionth the size of a human brain.

A dragonfly's compound eye contains as many as 30,000 lenses, while an ant's eye may have fewer than 150 lenses.

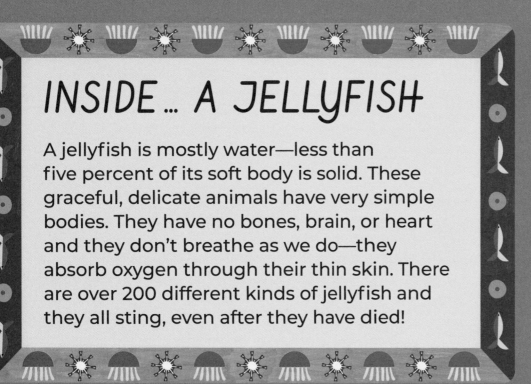

INSIDE ... A JELLYFISH

A jellyfish is mostly water—less than five percent of its soft body is solid. These graceful, delicate animals have very simple bodies. They have no bones, brain, or heart and they don't breathe as we do—they absorb oxygen through their thin skin. There are over 200 different kinds of jellyfish and they all sting, even after they have died!

Life cycle

Jellyfish make eggs that develop into anemone-like forms, called polyps. These polyps settle down on a solid surface such as a rock. Eventually, the polyps produce young jellyfish, which float away and grow into adult jellyfish that live for about three to six months.

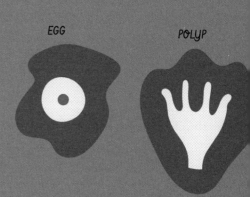

EGG

POLYP

Nerve net

Without a brain, jellyfish rely on a simple network of nerves to automatically detect light, touch, and smells, and to respond to their surroundings. Some jellyfish also detect light with simple eye spots around the edge of their bell.

Movement

Most jellyfish save energy by drifting with the wind or water currents. Some swim slowly by using muscles to open and close their bell like an umbrella in a steady rhythm. This forces water in and out of the bell and pushes the jellyfish along.

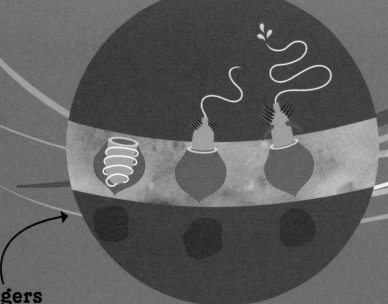

Stingers

Jellyfish stingers have a coiled thread inside that unwinds and shoots out of the tentacles, injecting poison into a victim like a tiny dart. The poisonous injections stun prey so that the jellyfish can easily pull it into its mouth.

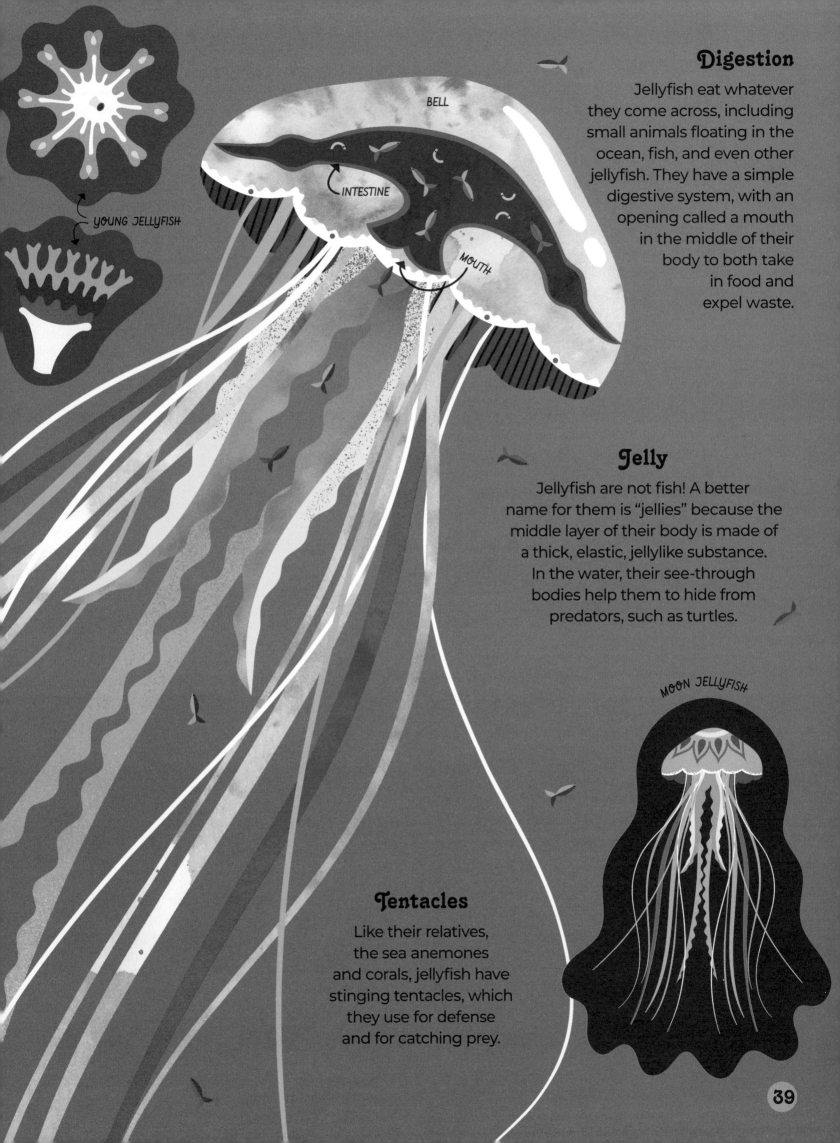

YOUNG JELLYFISH

BELL

INTESTINE

MOUTH

Digestion

Jellyfish eat whatever they come across, including small animals floating in the ocean, fish, and even other jellyfish. They have a simple digestive system, with an opening called a mouth in the middle of their body to both take in food and expel waste.

Jelly

Jellyfish are not fish! A better name for them is "jellies" because the middle layer of their body is made of a thick, elastic, jellylike substance. In the water, their see-through bodies help them to hide from predators, such as turtles.

MOON JELLYFISH

Tentacles

Like their relatives, the sea anemones and corals, jellyfish have stinging tentacles, which they use for defense and for catching prey.

INSIDE... AN ELEPHANT

The African elephant is the largest and heaviest animal living on land today. A large male weighs as much as 80 people. African elephants also have the largest ears of any animal—they are as big as tablecloths! Asian elephants have smaller ears. Flapping their ears back and forth helps elephants to cool down.

Big brain

Elephants are very intelligent animals with a good memory. Their brain is about four times bigger than a human brain.

Giant intestines

Elephant intestines can weigh nearly a ton. Elephants eat more than 100 different plants and spend about 16 hours a day choosing, picking, and eating their food.

STOMACH

Heart

An elephant's heart is about five times bigger than a human heart and weighs as much as a small child. It beats about 30 times a minute, which is less than half your heart rate.

AFRICAN ELEPHANT

Tusks

An elephant's tusks are its two long front teeth. Tusks grow all through an elephant's life, at a rate of about 6 inches a year. An elephant uses its tusks mainly for feeding, but also as a weapon.

Tube trunk

An elephant's trunk is made up of more than 40,000 muscles —you have only about 650 muscles in your whole body! An elephant uses its trunk to breathe, eat, squirt water, and make sounds.

BRAIN

LUNGS

Fatty feet

A fatty pad inside an elephant's heel cushions the massive weight of its body, spreading out as the elephant puts its foot down. Thick, strong bones inside the elephant's legs support its body like the pillars of a building.

Grinding teeth

Inside an elephant's mouth are four huge molar teeth. Each tooth weighs more than a brick! Sharp ridges on these molar teeth help to grind up tough plant food.

INSIDE ... A HONEYBEE

Most of the 60,000 honeybees in an average beehive are female worker bees. They collect food, take care of the young, guard the hive and make wax sheets called honeycombs. Honeybees store honey in the hive to feed their young and to help them survive the winter, huddling together to keep warm.

Beeswax

Worker honeybees produce flakes of beeswax under their abdomens. They chew the wax flakes in their mouths to soften them and use them to build sheets of six-sided honeycombs.

Sting

A honeybee stings to defend the hive from predators, or when it is scared. It pumps poison (venom) into its victims through a sharp, hollow sting at the end of its abdomen. A honeybee can only sting once—when it does, it dies.

HEART

INTESTINE

HONEY STOMACH

AIR SAC

WAX

HONEYBEE

Pollen basket

On their back legs, honeybees have stiff, strong, curved hairs, which make a "basket" for holding the yellow pollen they collect from flowers. Bees mix plant pollen with water to make "bee bread," which they feed to their developing young (larvae).

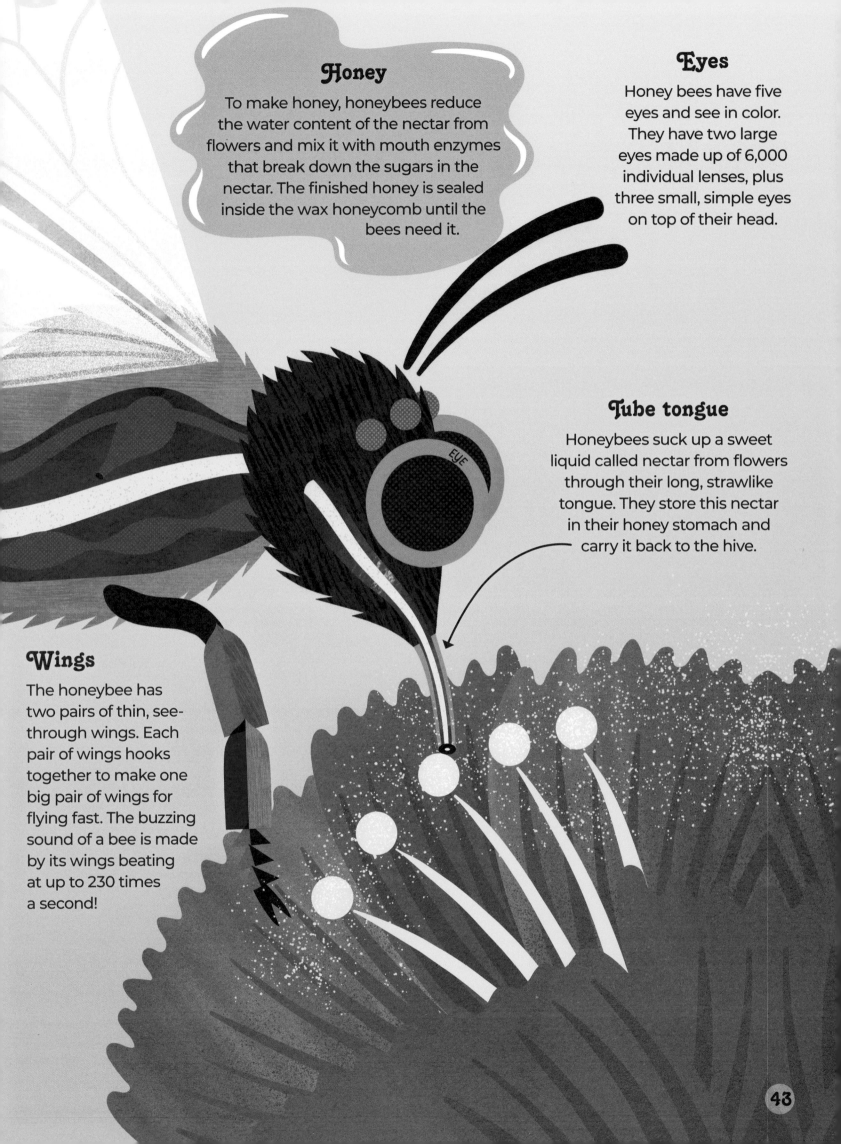

Honey

To make honey, honeybees reduce the water content of the nectar from flowers and mix it with mouth enzymes that break down the sugars in the nectar. The finished honey is sealed inside the wax honeycomb until the bees need it.

Eyes

Honey bees have five eyes and see in color. They have two large eyes made up of 6,000 individual lenses, plus three small, simple eyes on top of their head.

Tube tongue

Honeybees suck up a sweet liquid called nectar from flowers through their long, strawlike tongue. They store this nectar in their honey stomach and carry it back to the hive.

Wings

The honeybee has two pairs of thin, see-through wings. Each pair of wings hooks together to make one big pair of wings for flying fast. The buzzing sound of a bee is made by its wings beating at up to 230 times a second!

HEART AND BLOOD

In most animals, blood transports nutrients and gases through the body. The blood often flows through a system of narrow tubes, called blood vessels. It is kept moving by one or more pumps, called hearts. In some animals, such as insects and shellfish, the blood moves slowly through open spaces in the body, rather than through blood vessels.

What is a heart?

In some animals, a heart is an expanded blood vessel with a thick, muscular wall. In other animals, the heart is a more complex structure with two, three, or even four sections called chambers inside.

Two chambers

A fish's heart has only two chambers inside. One chamber collects blood from the body and the other chamber pumps blood to the gills, where it picks up oxygen. The blood then goes around the rest of the fish's body before going back to the heart.

Four chambers

Birds and mammals have a very efficient heart with four chambers. This pumps blood containing lots of oxygen through the body and sends blood low in oxygen back to the lungs. The blood moves around the body in two separate loops, rather than in just one loop, as happens in a fish.

1 Heart rate

To help digestion, some snakes can make their hearts swell to almost twice normal size. This pumps more blood with each heartbeat, and helps to release energy from the snake's meal. The heart shrinks back to its original size afterward.

2 Number of hearts

Most animals have one heart, like humans. A few animals, however, have several hearts. Octopuses and squid have up to three hearts, hagfish have four hearts, and earthworms have five pairs of heartlike structures!

3 No heart

Some animals don't need a heart to pump blood containing oxygen and nutrients around their bodies. These are usually simple animals, such as starfish, sponges, flatworms, and sea anemones, which can take in oxygen and nutrients all over their body surface.

4 Insect blood

Inside an insect's body, blood moves around in a big space, rather than being enclosed in narrow blood vessels. The blood is kept moving by the heart, which sucks in blood through little holes in its sides and pumps it out through a hole at the front.

5 Tubes for blood

In all animals with backbones, the heart pumps blood around the body through a network of blood vessels. Blood vessels carrying blood away from the heart are called arteries. Blood vessels carrying blood back to the heart are called veins.

6 Blood color

Animals may have red, blue, green, yellow, orange, violet, or colorless blood. The reason for the colors may be due to the pigments used to carry oxygen in the blood. It may also be due to waste products from breaking down food, or to chemicals taken in by, or made by, the animals themselves.

Did you know?

You would need a microscope to see the heart of the fairy fly, a type of wasp that's less than 0.2 mm long.

If a zebrafish's heart is injured, it can quickly repair itself so it is working well again.

The human heart is about the size of a person's fist. It beats 100,000 times a day.

INSIDE... A SEA TURTLE

The seven different kinds of sea turtles live in all of the world's oceans, although females have to come onto land to lay their eggs. The largest, the giant leatherbacks, are as long as a grown adult. Sea turtles have a flat, streamlined shell and strong front flippers that help them swim as fast as 21 miles per hour.

Breathing

Sea turtles have to come to the surface of the ocean to breathe air into their lungs. They use muscles between their front legs to draw air in and out of the body. They can hold their breath underwater for four to seven hours.

Eggs

Female sea turtles use their back flippers to dig a nesting hole on a beach, which is often the same beach used by their own mothers. They lay more than 100 eggs at a time. The eggs are the size of table tennis balls, but have soft, flexible shells.

INTESTINE

Shell

Most sea turtles have a bony shell on their backs as well as underneath their bodies. On top of the bony shell are waterproof giant scales, or scutes. They are made of keratin, just like your fingernails.

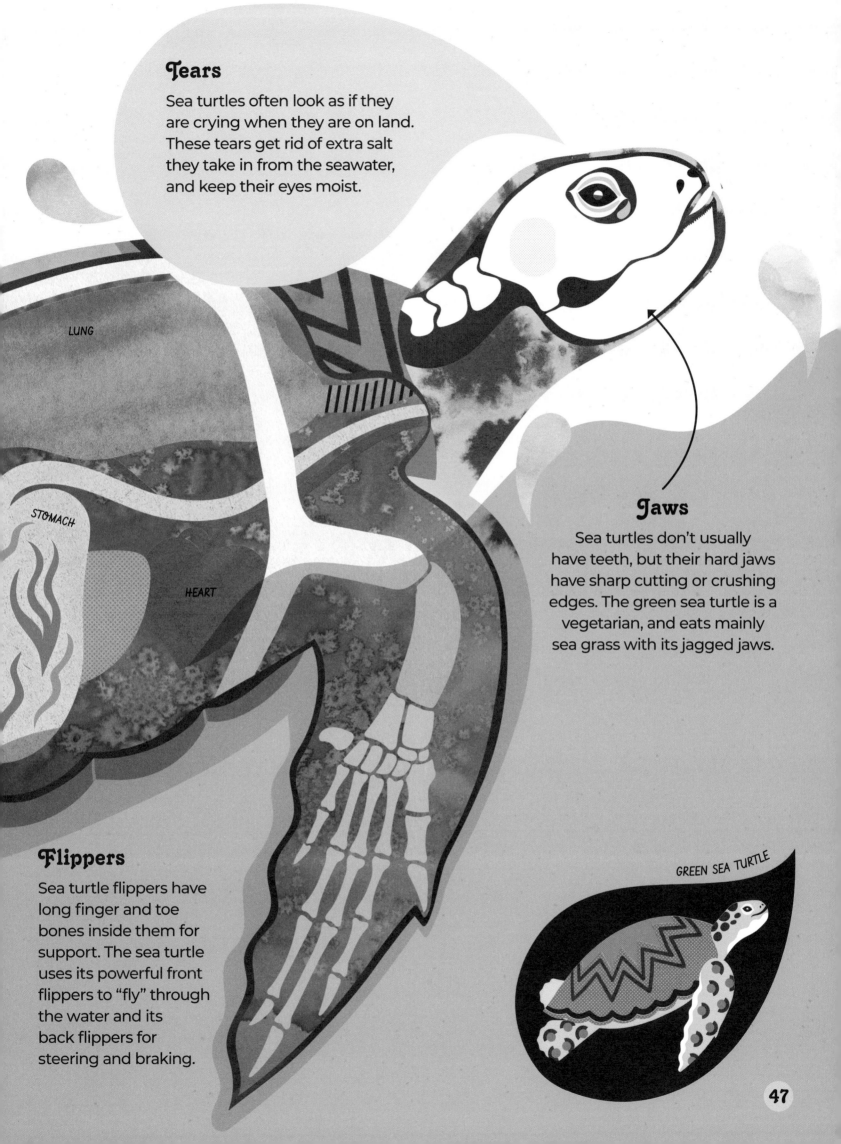

Tears

Sea turtles often look as if they are crying when they are on land. These tears get rid of extra salt they take in from the seawater, and keep their eyes moist.

LUNG

STOMACH

HEART

Jaws

Sea turtles don't usually have teeth, but their hard jaws have sharp cutting or crushing edges. The green sea turtle is a vegetarian, and eats mainly sea grass with its jagged jaws.

Flippers

Sea turtle flippers have long finger and toe bones inside them for support. The sea turtle uses its powerful front flippers to "fly" through the water and its back flippers for steering and braking.

GREEN SEA TURTLE

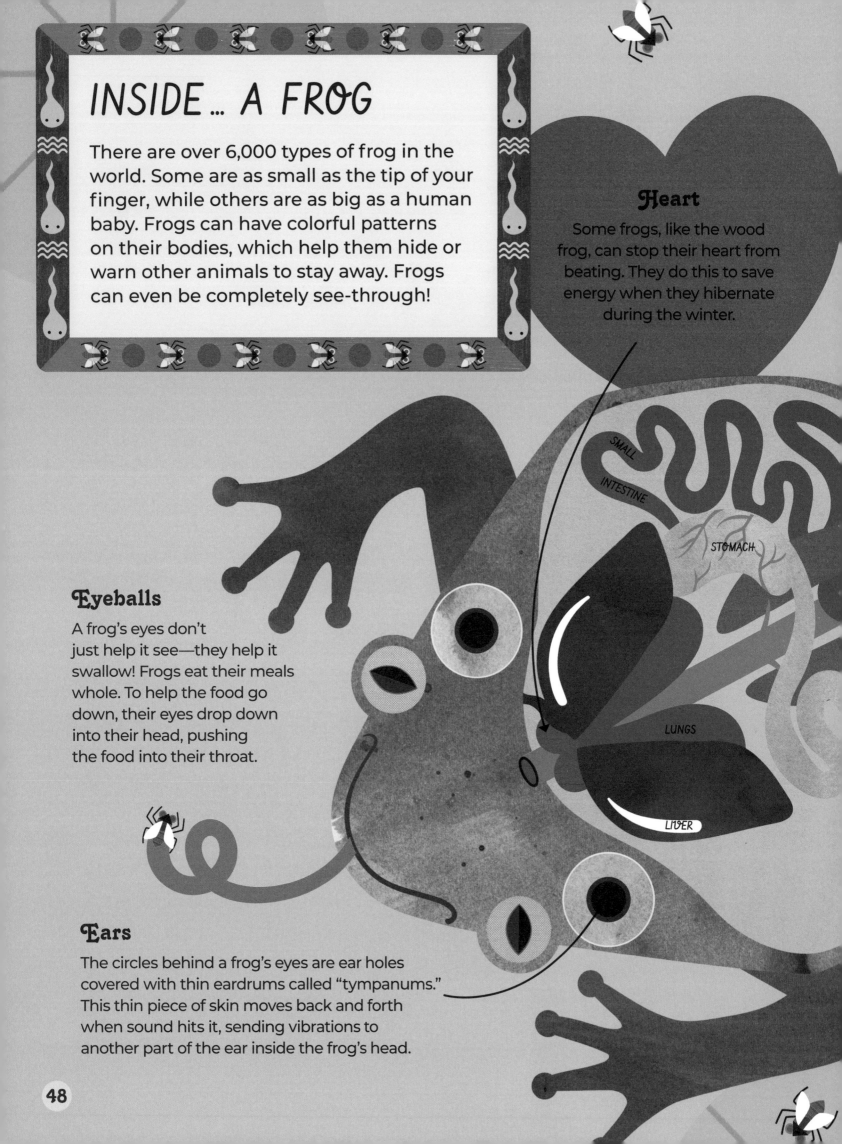

INSIDE ... A FROG

There are over 6,000 types of frog in the world. Some are as small as the tip of your finger, while others are as big as a human baby. Frogs can have colorful patterns on their bodies, which help them hide or warn other animals to stay away. Frogs can even be completely see-through!

Heart

Some frogs, like the wood frog, can stop their heart from beating. They do this to save energy when they hibernate during the winter.

SMALL INTESTINE

STOMACH

LUNGS

LIVER

Eyeballs

A frog's eyes don't just help it see—they help it swallow! Frogs eat their meals whole. To help the food go down, their eyes drop down into their head, pushing the food into their throat.

Ears

The circles behind a frog's eyes are ear holes covered with thin eardrums called "tympanums." This thin piece of skin moves back and forth when sound hits it, sending vibrations to another part of the ear inside the frog's head.

Skin

Frogs don't use their mouths to drink water. Instead, they take it in through their skin! On their legs and bellies, there are patches of skin that absorb water.

TREE FROG

Big jumper

Frogs are super hoppers! Their legs have extra joints that allow them to bend easily. A frog powers its jumps by bending its long legs close to the body and then stretching them out straight.

LARGE INTESTINE

Long toes

Frogs' long, webbed toes are perfect for swimming. Their paddle-shaped feet help them push themselves easily through water.

Lungs

When frogs hear or make sounds, their lungs vibrate just as their earss do. This helps frogs pinpoint the source of a sound. It also helps to make their calls quieter so they don't hurt their ears with their own noisy croaking.

INSIDE... A GIRAFFE

Giraffes are the tallest land animals living today. They grow up to 20 feet tall with a neck nearly six feet long. This extra-long neck allows giraffes to feed from high branches on trees and to spot danger. It also helps males fight each other and win a mate.

Hairy horns

Male and female giraffes have pairs of hairy "horns" called ossicones, which means "bony cone." They are born with ossicones, which lie flat during birth to avoid injury. The ossicones may help with temperature control. Males also fight with their horns when competing for females.

Bendy neck

Surprisingly, a giraffe has only seven bones inside its long neck—the same number as you do! However, each giraffe neck bone can be over 9 in long. The neck bones are also linked together with ball-and-socket joints, like your shoulder joints. This makes a giraffe's neck super-bendy.

Long tongue

A giraffe's thick, grasping tongue is so long it can lick its nose! The black tip stops the tongue from getting sunburned while the giraffe reaches for leaves. Thick, sticky saliva inside the mouth coats any sharp thorns that the giraffe might swallow.

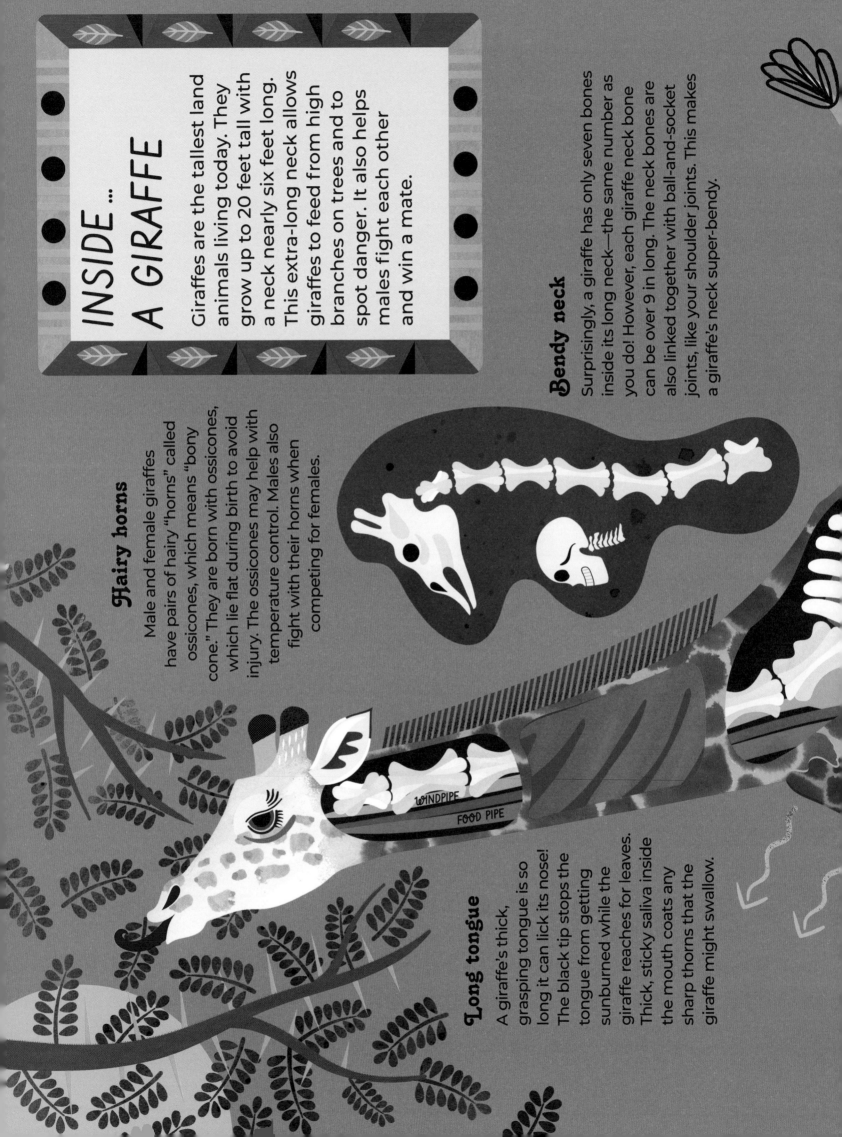

WINDPIPE

FOOD PIPE

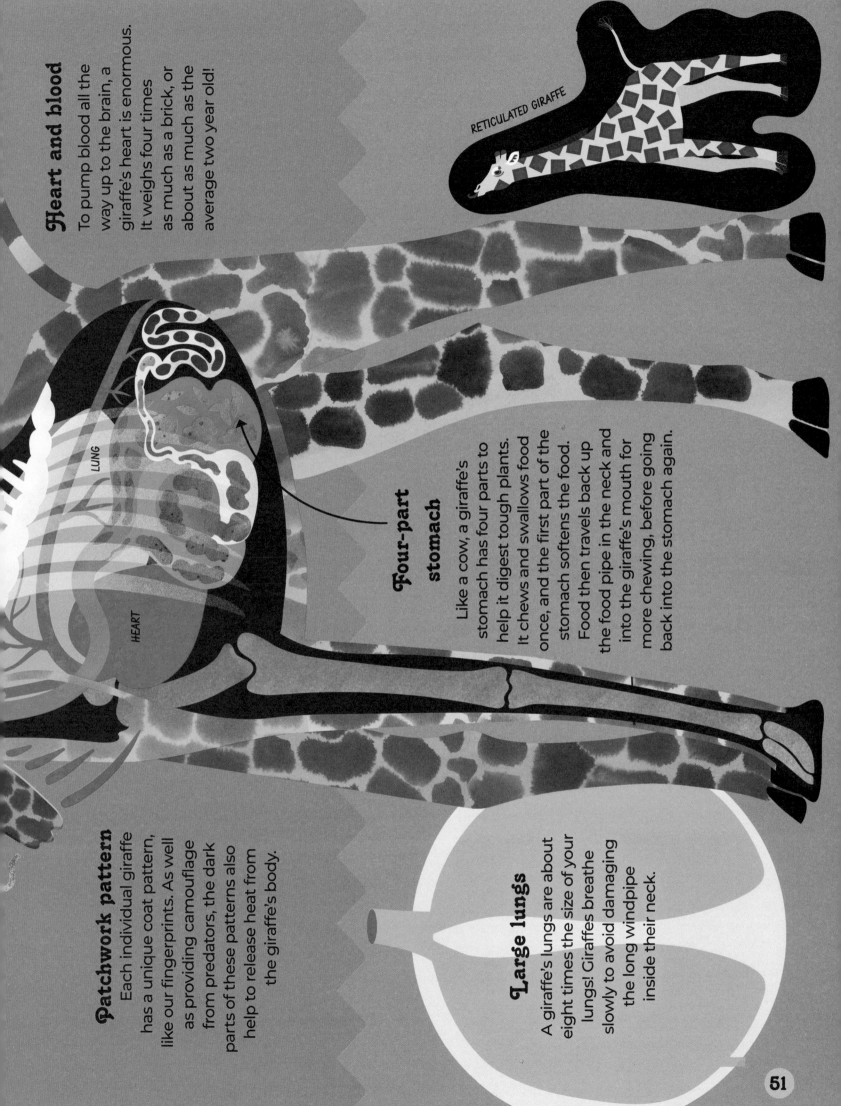

Heart and blood

To pump blood all the way up to the brain, a giraffe's heart is enormous. It weighs four times as much as a brick, or about as much as the average two year old!

RETICULATED GIRAFFE

LUNG

HEART

Four-part stomach

Like a cow, a giraffe's stomach has four parts to help it digest tough plants. It chews and swallows food once, and the first part of the stomach softens the food. Food then travels back up the food pipe in the neck and into the giraffe's mouth for more chewing, before going back into the stomach again.

Patchwork pattern

Each individual giraffe has a unique coat pattern, like our fingerprints. As well as providing camouflage from predators, the dark parts of these patterns also help to release heat from the giraffe's body.

Large lungs

A giraffe's lungs are about eight times the size of your lungs! Giraffes breathe slowly to avoid damaging the long windpipe inside their neck.

AMAZING ORGANS

An animal's body is usually made up of different microscopic (tiny) units called cells. Groups of the same type of cells are called tissues. In a complex animal, tissues are joined together to form organs, such as the brain, eye, or heart, which have different jobs to do. Some animals have unusual or amazing organs that help them to survive.

❶ Electric organs

Fish called electric rays make and store electricity in kidney-shaped organs near their front fins. They can produce electric shocks of between 14 and 220 volts to stun prey, defend themselves, and communicate.

❷ Giant eyes

The giant squid has the biggest eyes of any animal—they are at least 9 in across, as big as soccer balls or dinner plates! These giant eyes help the squid to look out for predators, such as sperm whales.

❸ Glow-in-the-dark

Many creatures glow in the inky blackness of the deep ocean. Some have "light organs"—organs that produce light with the help of chemical reactions or special bacteria. Glowing in the dark helps animals to find prey, defend themselves, or signal to others.

❹ Biggest brain

A sperm whale has the largest and heaviest brain, weighing around 19 pounds—about twice as heavy as a cat.

❺ Singing birds

Songbirds sing using an organ called the syrinx, located where their windpipe joins the tubes leading to the lungs. A thin membrane inside the syrinx vibrates to produce sounds, and songbirds use special muscles to control this organ.

❻ Big hearts, small hearts

The smaller the animal, the faster its heart works to force blood through its tiny blood vessels. The gigantic blue whale's heart beats at nine to ten beats per minute, whereas a shrew (small enough to fit in your hand) has a heart rate of over 1,000 beats per minute.

❼ Air exchange

When dolphins breathe in air, they can exchange 80 percent of the old air in their lungs for fresh air. This helps them to hold their breath underwater for up to seven minutes. Humans can only exchange 17 percent of the air in their lungs when they take a breath.

❽ Special sponges

Sponges have no tissues or organs, so they have no muscles, nervous system, or blood system. These simple animals have bodies that contain just two layers of cells.

❾ Stretched-out snakes

Inside a snake's stretched-out body, there is not much room for its organs. So a snake's organs, such as its liver, kidneys, and stomach, are a long, thin shape. Most snakes have only one long, thin right lung, which does the work of two lungs.

Did you know?

A buzzard can see its prey from a height of nearly 15,000 feet. Its eye has 1 million photoreceptors—cells that respond to light.

Drum fish make loud drumming noises with muscles that vibrate against their swim bladder (an air-filled sac).

The scallop has 100 eyes around the edge of its shell.

INTESTINE

STOMACH

LIVER

Silent feathers

The flight feathers of an owl are soft and velvety, which helps it to swoop silently down onto its prey. In some owls, the feathers near the tips of the wings have comblike edges that muffle the sound of the wings even further.

Bones

An owl's bones are strong and stiff. Many are hollow, with crisscross struts for strength so they don't break in flight. A large, flat breastbone supports powerful flight muscles. It also protects the organs underneath, such as the heart and lungs.

Pellets

Owls swallow their prey whole and can't digest every part, such as bones and fur. The undigested food is pressed together into large pellets that the owl then coughs up and spits out.

Twisty neck

Owls have 14 bones in their neck—twice as many as you do! This helps them to twist their neck nearly all the way around to look behind them.

BARN OWL

Bill

An owl uses its sharp, hooked bill to tear up its food into pieces small enough to swallow.

Enormous eyes

Owls have huge, tube-shaped eyes. They are fixed in place by bones, so they can't move on their own. The eyes face the front to help the owl judge distances accurately and see in 3D.

Terrible talons

An owl uses its large, needle-sharp, clasping claws, called talons, for catching its prey. Two of its talons move forward and two move backward to grip the prey very tightly and stop it escaping.

INSIDE... AN OWL

Most owls are nighttime hunters of small animals such as mice, voles, and insects. An owl can see two or three times better in the dark than you can. Its excellent eyesight and keen hearing helps it to catch its prey. There are over 200 different kinds of owl, including this barn owl, which has a dish-shaped face to help it collect sounds for hunting.

INSIDE... A SPIDER

Small and delicate creatures, spiders are known for spinning silk and having poisonous fangs. But most spider poison is too weak to harm humans. Many people think that spiders are insects, but spiders have eight legs and two body parts, whereas insects have six legs and three body parts. A spider's eight legs each have six joints, so a spider has 48 knees!

Eight eyes

Spiders have poor eyesight, although they can see things from close-up using their big eyes. Their small eyes can detect the movement of their prey from further away.

POISON SAC

STOMACH

Book lungs

Most spiders breathe through one pair of "book lungs." These are spaces full of air with a stack of thin flaps inside, like the pages of a book. Air passes into the spider's blood through the thin walls of the booklike flaps.

Fearsome fangs

Nearly all spiders inject poison, called venom, into their prey through two sharp fangs. The venom paralyzes or kills the prey. The spider then turns its food into a soggy soup and sucks it into its stomach.

Blue blood

A spider's blood contains a copper pigment that turns blue-green when it carries oxygen.

Heart

A spider's heart forces blood into two main tubes, called arteries. Blood pours out of the open ends of the arteries all over the spider's body, eventually going back through the book lungs to the heart again.

HEART

INTESTINES

SILK GLANDS

Outer skeleton

The outside of a spider's body is protected by a hard exoskeleton. This can't stretch as the spider grows, so the spider climbs out of its old exoskeleton and stretches a soft new exoskeleton before it hardens. This process is called molting.

Spinning silk

Spiders pull silk out of structures called spinnerets in their abdomen. Spider silk is stronger than steel wire of the same thickness! It is used for making webs, wrapping prey and eggs, or even as a safety line. One teaspoon of spider silk would make a million webs.

Hairy spiders

Spiders rely on their sensitive hairs to collect information about food and danger from vibrations and smells in the air. Movement of the hairs triggers nerve signals that go to the spider's brain.

GARDEN SPIDER

57

INSIDE... A SCORPION

Scorpions have lived on Earth for over 400 million years—long before the dinosaurs! These ancient relatives of spiders are nighttime predators of insects, which they paralyze or kill with their poisonous sting. Scorpions are champion survivors and can live for a year without food, as long as they have water.

Baby carrier

Female scorpions give birth to baby scorpions. They are soft and white at first and cannot sting or feed. The babies ride around on their mother's back, where they are protected for about two to four weeks, after which the babies usually leave to fend for themselves.

HEART

BOOK LUNG

Stinger

At the tip of a scorpion's "tail" is a sharp, dagger-like needle, which injects venom for catching prey, or for defense.

Breathing

Small openings called spiracles on the outside of each body segment allow air to reach the scorpion's book lungs. Oxygen passes into the scorpion's blood through the "pages" of the book lungs, which work in a similar way to a fish's gills.

Glow in the dark

Scorpions absorb invisible ultraviolet light from the night sky and turn it into a blue-green glow. Scientists aren't sure why scorpions glow in the dark, but they may use ultraviolet light at night to find prey or shelter.

Legs and pincers

A scorpion has eight jointed legs, like its spider relatives. It also has big, crablike pincers on its head, which it uses to grab and hold its prey, ready for stinging or eating.

PINCER

BRAIN

INTESTINE

Molting

A scorpion's body is covered by a tough, leathery, waterproof exoskeleton. To grow larger, scorpions have to crack open this body armor, pull their body out of it, and stretch to a bigger size while their exoskeleton is still soft. This is called molting.

BARK SCORPION

GLOSSARY

Abdomen

The part of an animal's body that contains its digestive and reproductive organs.

Air sac

A space filled with air.

Backbone (spine)

A flexible chain of bones or cartilage (called vertebrae) between the skull and the tail of animals. It provides support and protection, and allows movement.

Bacteria

A group of microscopic living things made of one cell. Some are helpful, but others are harmful and cause diseases.

Blubber

A thick layer of fat between the skin and the muscles of some animals, which helps to trap body heat and keeps them warm in cold places.

Bone

A strong, hard, living substance that forms the skeleton of humans and many other animals with backbones.

Breastbone (sternum)

A thin, flat bone in the middle of an animal's chest. The ribs join the breastbone to the backbone.

Camouflage

The colors and patterns on an animal's body that help it to blend in with its surroundings.

Cartilage

A tough, elastic substance.

Cells

The basic building blocks of all living things.

Chitin

A tough substance that is the main ingredient in the exoskeletons of insects, spiders, scorpions, and the shells of crabs.

Digestion

The process of breaking down food to release its nutrients in a form that can be absorbed into an animal's body.

Enzyme

A substance that speeds up the rate of a chemical reaction in a living thing, without itself being changed in the process.

Exoskeleton

A shell or a hard skeleton covering the outside of an animal's body.

Gills

Structures that animals, such as fish, use for breathing underwater.

Gizzard

A muscular chamber in the food tube of some animals, such as birds and insects. The gizzard helps to grind up food.

Gland

An organ in an animal's body. A gland produces chemical substances for the body to use for a particular purpose, or to get rid of into its surroundings.

Intestine

The tube through which food passes when it leaves an animal's stomach.

Keratin

A tough protein in the outer layers of animals' skin. Hoofs, nails, claws, bills, horns, hair, and feathers are all made mainly of keratin.

Larva (plural: larvae)

An active, wingless stage, such as a caterpillar, in the development of many animals.

Lens

A transparent structure inside an animal's eye that focuses light on the back of the eye.

Liver

A large, complex organ in the abdomen of animals with backbones. The liver cleans the blood of harmful substances, processes and stores foods and makes bile, which helps the intestine to absorb fats.

Mammal

An animal with fur or hair, such as a human or a cow. Mammals are warm-blooded and feed their young on mother's milk.

Mantle

A muscular structure that forms the outer wall of a mollusck's body and encloses its internal organs like a cloak.

Membrane

A thin, flexible layer of material, which forms a barrier or a lining.

Molting

The shedding of an animal's outer covering, such as skin, feathers, hair, or a hard shell or exoskeleton.

Nectar

A sweet liquid produced by flowers to attract the animals they need to carry their pollen to other flowers.

Nerve

A bundle of fibers that uses electrical signals to send information rapidly around an animal's body.

Nose leaf

A leaf-shaped flap, or fold of skin, on a bat's nose, which may help it to send the sounds it makes in different directions.

Organ

A part or a structure in an animal that does a special job, such as the heart, stomach, or lungs.

Pigment

A chemical used to make a color.

Pollen

A fine yellow dust produced by the male parts of seed plants. Pollen needs to travel from the male part to the female part of a flower so that seeds can develop.

Predator

An animal that hunts and eats other animals for food.

Prey

An animal that is killed and eaten by another animal.

Reptile

An animal with a backbone and scaly skin, which breathes air. Reptiles include snakes, turtles, and crocodiles.

Streamlined

Something that is a smooth, pointy shape, which helps it to move easily through air or water.

Swim bladder

A sac full of air inside most bony fish. It helps these fish to control their position under the water by stopping them from rising or sinking.

Ultraviolet light

Invisible rays that are part of the energy that comes from the sun and are reflected by the moon at night.

Valve

A device for stopping or controlling the flow of a liquid, gas, or other material by opening or closing passageways. The elastic flaps in blood vessels are a type of valve.

Vocal cords

Folds of skin in the throat of some animals, which vibrate and produce sound when air passes over them.

Warm-blooded

Animals that are able to keep their body at the same warm temperature, no matter how warm or cool their surroundings are.

Windpipe

The tubelike pipe, or airway, which connects the throat to the lungs.

INDEX